My Body

Contents

This is my head.

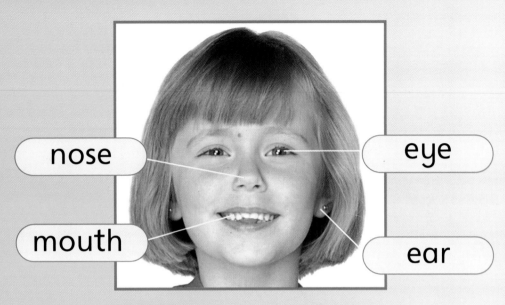

nose

eye

mouth

ear

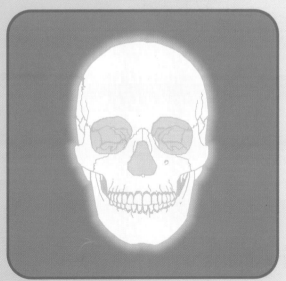

This is my chest.

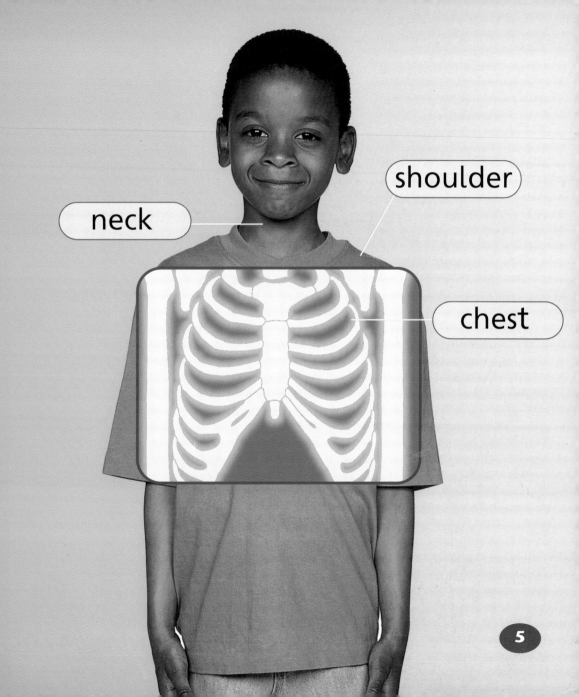

neck

shoulder

chest

5

This is my arm and hand.

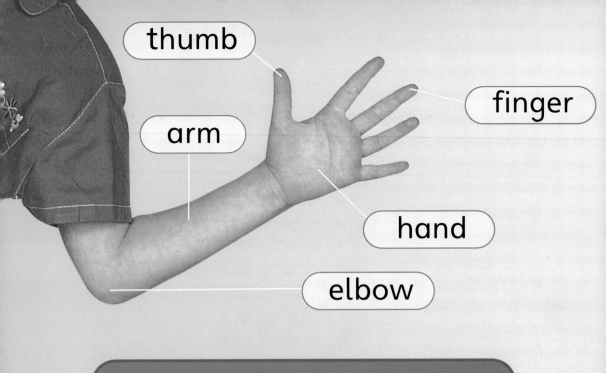

thumb

finger

arm

hand

elbow

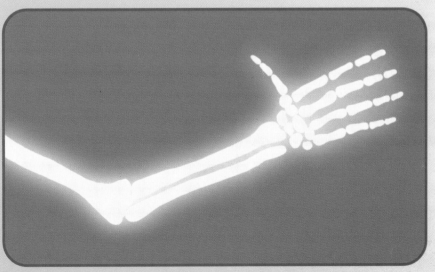

This is my leg and foot.

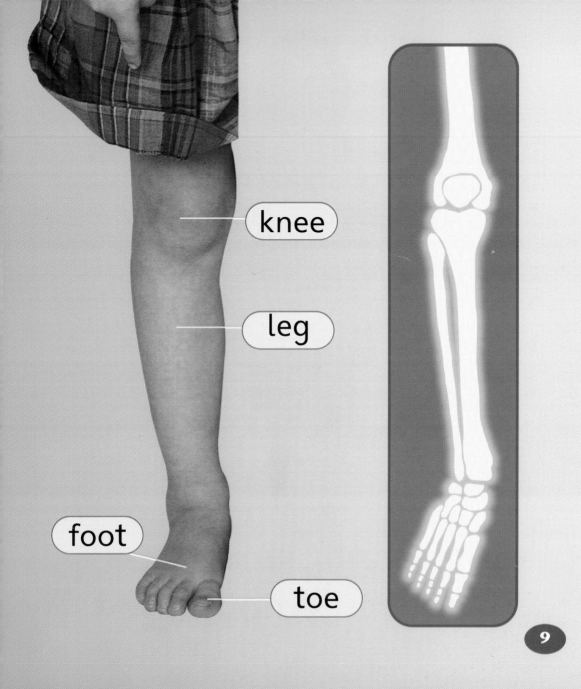

knee

leg

foot

toe

This is my whole body.

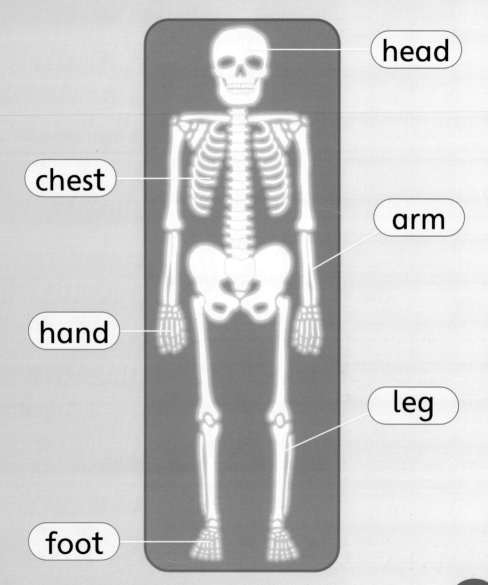

head

chest

arm

hand

leg

foot

Index

a
b
c
d
e
f
g
h
i
j
k
l
m
n
o
p
q
r
s
t
u
v
w
x
y
z